PRINCIPLES TO SAFEGUARD YOUR MARRIAGE

TOM EDWARDS

First edition .

TABLE OF CONTENTS

INTRODUCTION

In our present world, many wedded individuals are unsettled in their relationships. Cheating and lying blended in with terrible way of behaving have flip around marriage. Many variables have added to the reason for misery in marriage.

The pith of marriage isn't just for procreation however to find fulfillment, satisfaction and love. Do you actually feel the affection you felt when\ you first expressed yes to him. Is the fire of adoration actually consuming in your marriage?

Numerous relationships are separating these days because of absence of care and commitment in the relationship. In the event that you can deal with your marriage the manner in which you deal with your body, you will partake in your marriage. Dealing with your marriage ought not be the obligation of one individual; rather is the obligation of the two people that have met up to fabricate major areas of strength for a superior future together. In marriage where one individual is all around committed and the other individual is going about as though is nothing of him should be concerned about, the relationship might self-destruct.

The social nature in man will continuously want to communicate with his kindred people, cooperation that is absent any trace of squabbles, misconception and malignancy. People are social and profound creatures that needs to adore and be cherished. In our the present reality where love and contempt are the two significant powers contradicting one another, we will continuously find satisfaction when we stick to love.

It requires work to safeguard, sustain, and grow a marriage. Between work timetables, kids, and different commitments, now and again it can appear to be difficult to keep up with that organization. At the point when issues emerge, a few couples see that as it's better to separate and go their different ways.1 For other people, dealing with the relationship is a superior decision. If you have any desire to remain with your partner and keep away from separate, there are proactive measures you can take from further developing correspondence to imbuing more sentiment into everyday life.

Anything of significant worth should be safeguarded - and your marriage is certainly important! To safeguard your relationship it's wise to keep your eyes open, impart well, and have some standard procedures to remain focused and safe. We live in a fallen world and enticement frequently crawls up unobtrusively. Each marriage has various conditions and difficulties, however there are normal peril zones we are undeniably presented to.

HEALTHY MARRIAGE

How can you say whether your marriage is healthy or not? This is an inquiry that is positively worth investigating, particularly assuming you have been pondering along those lines.

Similarly as it is all set for an ordinary actual examination with your doctor, so it is likewise great to have a relationship well-being examination occasionally to decide whether it qualifies as a decent marriage.

You might be very amazed or stunned when you hear what your pulse and cholesterol readings are, despite the fact that you had not thought that anything was wrong.

Essentially, when you investigate your marriage well-being, you might be in for a couple of shocks.

What does a Healthy marriage resemble

It takes a ton to have a blissful and sound marriage. The mystery lies in healthy relationship habits and not grand romantic gestures.

By taking an outline of indications of a cheerful marriage, you will actually want to step through a clear exam of your conjugal well-being, rescue your marriage from habits that are starving it from joy, and give the relationship a backbone.

In the event that as a couple you are in it for a long stretch, you should do a marriage registration with relevant inquiries like, "what makes a decent marriage?" "Are there any clear indications of a decent relationship?"

The following signs of a healthy marriage will give you an idea as to whether or not you enjoy a strong marriage.

1. They develop solid self-acknowledgment.

One of the critical indications of a decent marriage is developing solid self-acknowledgment

The most important move towards being a decent spouse is to acknowledge yourself. One of the vital indications of a decent marriage is developing solid self-acknowledgment.

At the point when you focus on appreciating and embracing yourself completely alongside your assets and shortcomings, it's an ideal marriage sign. It likewise makes a solid marriage, as self-acknowledgment works on our connections.

Fundamentally, you really want to have a decent connection with yourself, before you can hope to have a decent connection with another person.

This goes for all relationships , however particularly in marriage, truth be told. On the off chance that you regret yourself and you are anticipating that your life partner should meet all emotional and self-esteem needs, this is putting an irrational and ridiculous weight on your mate.

Sometimes you will be frustrated and afterward you will feel far and away more terrible. At the point when you acknowledge yourself as you are, as a work underway, your inspiration will be to give instead of get, to cherish and help, as opposed to need and need.

Astonishingly, with such a demeanor you typically turn out to be honored in kind, above and beyond.

2. They take full commitment for their own emotions.

Feelings assume such a crucial part in our lives consistently. They add tone to our connections - both splendid and grave tones, positive and negative.

The sound method for encountering feelings in marriage is when the two accomplices assume complete commitment for their own feelings, without accusing one another, and requesting that their accomplice meets their feelings.

Blaming is a most loved strategy of abusers who frequently say "You caused me to make it happen… " It is hazardous to overlook sentiments and stuff them down as opposed to confronting the issue and managing them out in the open.

Gloomy sentiments that have been full into the storm cellar of our souls don't mystically vanish - they rot and might in fact bring about "blasts" which cause hopelessness and grief, in some cases into the indefinite future.

Individuals attempt a wide range of things to balance their gloomy feelings, frequently prompting addictions and impulses. In an healthy marriage, feelings are communicated straightforwardly and unreservedly, as and when they happen.

One of the signs your marriage will last is the commonness of open, legit and straightforward communication in your relationship.

3. They set and maintain healthy boundaries.

Having firm limits that are unblemished and all around kept up with is one sign of positive marriage wellness.

The most important move towards solid limits is sorting out what precisely your limits are.

This is different for every individual and in a marriage, every mate has to know their very own limits, as well as their common limits as a team.

This covers for the most part, every region from finance to individual space, diet or assets. Limits additionally should be conveyed obviously to the one concerned, and when infringement happen, it depends on you to make a proper move.

For instance, on the off chance that you loan cash to somebody, saying that you need it returned in no less than a month, in the event that that doesn't occur, you would know not to loan to that individual once more.

4. They deal with conflicts as a team.

Indeed, having healthy conflicts is conceivable! If someone says, "we have no contentions by any means in our marriage," that would be cause for serious concern and uncertainty regarding the marriage's emotional wellness.

In such a case, there is either all out disregard or one accomplice is absolutely consistent and accommodating to the ruling one. Conflict is unavoidable when two totally unique and separate people choose to carry on with their lives in proximity and closeness.

Sound struggle happens when the issues are tended to, without going after the individual and character of your cherished one.

In Healthy conflict, the emphasis is on managing the issue and fixing the relationship. It's not necessary to focus on winning the contention or scoring focuses. It's tied in with defeating an impediment so you can develop considerably more like each other than you were previously.

The best indication of a sound relationship is your capacity as a team to settle issues collectively.

You might see what is going on in an unexpected way, however when you see and hear your accomplice's perspective, you are willing to walk that extra mile and meet the middle ground.

5. They have a great time together.

Marriage is solid when you can have a good time together and you anticipate being with your life partner and doing things you appreciate with one another.

At times wedded life can turn out to be so furiously occupied thus loaded with pressure and strain that the element of fun is lost.

This is a terrible misfortune, and each work ought to be made to recover a portion of the energy and cheerful fun that you might have delighted in toward the start of your relationship.

Pursue a class together or go ice-skating, or watch a parody together, and bring some sound fun into your marriage.

6. They support one another.

What makes an extraordinary marriage?

In a sound marriage, a couple is upheld by an accomplice who tunes in, regards, offers, and practices transparent correspondence. They exhibit a willingness to compromise and are open to constructive criticism.

Having a decent support structure in your marriage is crucial for a sound relationship. At the point when a couple become separate and segregated to the degree that they have not many external connections, it is an unfortunate sign.

Oppressive connections are quite often portrayed by isolation. The abuser isolate his mate so she believes she has "nobody to go to".

In a healthy marriage, both partners enjoy many and varied friendships with others, whether it is family members, fellow church members or work colleagues and friends.

7. They don't assume what their partner is thinking.

Refrain from rushing to make judgment or having assumptions about the thing your accomplice is thinking or feeling.

Take the initiative to inquire about the situation, to consider all points and don't accept what your accomplice is feeling show restraint while paying attention to them with no decisions.

As a couple, center around the context of the argument at hand, avoid making broad assumptions.

8. They mean it when they say sorry

Mature couples can perceive their role in their accomplice's torment.

They do not make a half-baked attempt at apologizing by saying, " I am sorry, you feel that way.."

Their conciliatory sentiment communicates sympathy and empathy for their accomplice, it mirrors their regret on the bad behaviors and shows that they will work at fixing the harm.

They find remedial ways to ensure it doesn't repeat.

9. They feel as though their partner is their safety net

Life tosses curve-balls consistently. One of the greatest benefits of a solid marriage is lounging in the solace of realizing somebody is there to watch your back.

In healthy marriages, successful couples aim at lessening the burden rather than adding to it. Your marriage is not in a good place, if all your spouse does is add to your woes or complicate an already difficult situation for you

They make their accomplice giggle at unimportant issues, and take a gander at a difficult circumstance from the shifted focal point of an amplifying glass, to diffuse its immensity.

In a blissful relationship, accomplices come to an agreement of arriving at an answer for an issue and not irritating it. They don't underestimate their accomplice and render close to home security to their mate.

10. Their sexual Life is flourishing

This is one is easy decision. Sex is significant, soothing and fun - all of this and more when a couple is partaking in a solid marriage.

I'm not saying sex is everything, or even that it is exaggerated. Be that as it may, underestimating sex in a marriage is definitely not an indication of a sound marriage.

On the off chance that the two accomplices are pleasing in a sexless marriage, it is a sad call of concern, nonetheless, assuming any of the accomplices is feeling baffled with absence of closeness in marriage, it can destroy the strength of the marriage and even lead to unfaithfulness.

Sex cultivates closeness and is the most private actual demonstration, you and your accomplice can insight to feel associated.

11. Their home is overflowing with positive energy

A healthy house is continuously overflowing with energy. There is consistently a buzz with a quality discussion or a tomfoolery chat occurring to and fro. You figure out how to interface with your life partner on horde points. You share superb genuine discussions, and there is areas of strength for an of close to home association and energy.

On the other hand, a quiet house with a quiet marriage is a terrible collusion. On the off chance that the lethal quiet is tainting your marriage, figure out how to interface with your soul mate.

Seek clarification on some things, interface on effective issues, excursions, kids, regular difficulties or even trade a survey on a film, to keep it light.

Here are some ice breakers for couples to reconnect.

12. They don’t hold on to grudges

One thing that separates a sound marriage from an unfortunate marriage is a couple's capacity to relinquish the unimportant issues.

Mistakes and fights are not exclusive to any marriage. It's not all bad, however it is similarly critical to not allow hatred to rot.

Cease from disgracing your accomplice for their oversight and let your activities show your adoration and understanding. The capacity to relinquish past offenses is the sign of an experienced couple.

Try not to be a complaint gatherer or a power grabber. Fruitful couples work through their disparities and push ahead with illustrations learned.

The best couples focus on a careful discussion where they express their issue, a goal to not repeat the slip-up, acknowledge the statement of regret, and let go, to keep embracing current circumstances.

Assuming you find that these strong marks of a sound marriage are absent to any extraordinary degree in your relationship, kindly don't overlook the warnings that you see and make sure to proficient assistance.

UNHEALTHY MARRIAGE

Each relationship has its personal recurring patterns. At the point when weariness sets in or emotions rage out of control, you might begin thinking about what has been going on with your fantasy ideal world. Consider the possibility that you pursued some unacceptable decision. Imagine a scenario where our marriage is undesirable. Consider the possibility that the individual you wedded isn't exactly the individual you wedded.

Indeed, Even the best of marriages explore predictable stages. Nobody can stay immersed in those animating, edgy sentiment until the end of time. Eventually, couples need to live, return to work, bring up children, manage crises, see loved ones.

Yet, that doesn't mean love can't be consistent and supported. What's more, when whether or not a marriage is unfortunate emerges, it means a lot to get back to this mindfulness. How can you say whether your sound marriage has become unfortunate? Furthermore, more regrettable yet, how can you say whether your unfortunate marriage has become totally poisonous?

A healthy marriage is grounded in friendship. Every companion thinks often about the prosperity and most elevated great of the other and acknowledges liability regarding his/her job when issues emerge. The marriage is an organization, not an enmeshment.

A healthy marriage upholds the uniqueness of every person, similarly as it supports the uniqueness of the actual association.

How would you measure in the event that your marriage is unhealthy? In the event that there were a thermometer for relationship well being, what might it be?

The most straightforward mark of the strength of a relationship is the means by which the partners communicate. You may not be holding tight each other each word any longer. However, on the off chance that you're not paying attention to or thinking often about what your companion says (or the other way around), you ought to be seeing a few warnings.

Communication shaves its direction into each part of a relationship. It goes past the verbally expressed word to what is implicit, expected, dreaded, felt, suggested. We are continuously discussing (even with ourselves). What makes a difference is the thing and how we're imparting and whether we have the mindfulness to perceive those fundamental relationship components.

Here are a few signs that your marriage is unhealthy (or is heading in that direction):

1. **You start blaming one another.**

It takes a great deal of energy to search inside yourself and assess where you might have improved in a circumstance. Furthermore, it takes a great deal of modesty and trust to offer an earnest expression of remorse and obligation to work harder for the benefit of your marriage.

Criticism becomes common. Criticism is an approach of going after someone else. It goes directly to the individual's personality, normally as "you generally/never" articulations. It is the section to a pattern of criticism and defensiveness, the two of which can rapidly dissolve a marriage.

Healthy relationships are secured in self-commitment. Life partners might have their altercations, yet they know how to fess up to their own downfalls.

At the point when communication begins getting thoughtless, mates aren't as inspired by the opposite's side of the story. It becomes simpler to avoid, evade, and open discourse with "you" articulations.

Furthermore, that turns into an extreme propensity to bring back in.

2. You stop spending meaningful time together.

Marriage requires a steady infusion of positive goal. Furthermore, when life gets jam-loaded with professions and kids, you might lose interest in planning time for you two.

While sex means a lot to the well-being of a marriage, it's not all that matters. Investing energy talking, arranging, going on dates, and attempting new things together are ways of building and secure closeness.

Assuming you notice that you've become more like avoidant room mates than a cheerfully married couple, you might have a sign that your marriage is unhealthy.

3. You avoid fighting.

This isn't a stunt explanation. Clearly, harmony is everybody's objective, even on the home front. Yet, individuals in sound relationships do battle. Why and how matters.

If you are changing your behavior or giving up on things that matter to you because you don't want to fight, pay attention. This pattern could be a red flag that bigger issues are going on.

Is it true that you fear your mate's attitude? Do you feel depleted simply contemplating what the fight will look like? Do you two not have rules about belligerence? Have you started abandoning your marriage?

4. One partner starts controlling the other.

Marriage should be an equivalent organization in which the two players bring their persuasions, needs, and needs to a similar table.

At the point when a marriage is undesirable, issues of control are generally clear. Finances are an easy weapon of control. One accomplice begins concluding how cash is spent and how much the other companion can spend.

At the point when one mate utilizes terrorizing, requests, or dangers to control what the other companion spends or does, the marriage might be harmful.

Control is one of the many indications of misuse, and it can drain over into each region of a relationship. Control can likewise pour out over into regions like friendship and outside activities.

5. You stop laughing together.

Laughing isn't simply great medication, it resembles Super Glue. Couples who giggle at themselves and at their own "relationship funnies" have a more profound closeness than the individuals who don't. Contemplate how your relationship and life overall would look on the off chance that you didn’t take yourself quite so seriously.

6. You start to feel isolated.

Control (and maltreatment overall) flourishes in a setting of detachment. Assuming you notice that your public activity has become non-existent, or on the other hand on the off chance that your mate disgraces you for your friendships, you have motivation to be concerned.

7. You have no voice.

In an healthy marriage, the two accomplices have an equivalent voice — in any event, when they conflict. Every individual's sentiments, needs, and needs matter as much as the other's.

In a harmful relationship, be that as it may, one accomplice is many times closed down and given no voice.

Your fundamental beliefs are completely different. In any event, when a marriage is unhealthy, mates might in any case have normal fundamental beliefs. They just may have failed to focus on the most proficient method to live them out with regards to the marriage.

Assuming your marriage has become harmful, you presumably don't have even the most fundamental things to clutch any longer. In the event that you're not in total agreement about basics like children, professions, and issues of confidence, having something to pursue is troublesome.

8. You feel as though you are losing yourself.

A sound marriage is rich ground for the confidence of the two accomplices to develop and be reinforced. At the point when you don't perceive yourself any longer, you might be in a poisonous, even harmful, relationship.

Both undesirable and poisonous connections are cause for sure fire activity. Looking for mediation can assist you with fixing an undesirable marriage and get that caring inclination back.

Fixing a totally poisonous marriage may not be imaginable. In any case just you and your companion can choose if it merits the work. Whether to remain in your hopeless marriage or separation is a hard choice. Yet, when there is mindfulness and assurance to develop, there is consistently trust.

The jump from "undesirable" to "harmful" may appear to be more similar to a scarcely discernible difference than a leap, particularly in the event that you don't focus on early signs.

In poisonous relationships, sensations of despondency are frequently combined with sensations of dread or potentially sadness.

SAFEGUARDING YOUR MARRIAGE

Your kids (in the event that you've brought them up in a solid manner) will one day venture out from home and begin their very own home. This doesn't mean you move away from them; it just shows your relationship changes.

In any case, your marriage is intended to endure forever. After the children are developed and gone, you will be left with your mate. Question is, would you say you are putting resources into your relationship such that future-safeguards it? Do you have shields set up to guarantee you have an incredible relationship after the kids are raised?

1. COMMUNICATING WITH YOUR PARTNER

Communication in relationships is like a river. When thoughts and feelings flow smoothly between marriage partners its fun, feel good, and help support everyone around. However, when communication flow is turbulent, it's potentially dangerous and destructive. And when communication gets blocked, pressure builds up. Then when the words start flowing again, they tend to come out suddenly in a damaging raging flood because many married couples struggle with healthy communication, especially about important issues. it’s common for couples to avoid difficult conversations They share trickles of information back and forth about who’s going where when and who’s going to pick up the kids, without ever diving into the conversations that are actually most important to them. Overtime, the lack of a full communication flow dries up the passion and love between them.

What does extraordinary marriage communication resemble?

In an extraordinary relationship couples talk unreservedly, transparently, and have a solid sense of security sharing their most confidential considerations. They serenely and kindly express their interests and sentiments when hardships emerge and voice their positive contemplation's when things are great. The two partners talk thoughtfully, staying far from attacking, destructive or controlling remarks. They listen mindfully, attempting to comprehend what their partner says with compassion as opposed to searching for what's up in what their partner needs to say or excusing what they hear, regardless of whether they have an alternate point of view. Furthermore, in the wake of talking, the two individuals in the marriage feel quite a bit better about the discussion, and feel like their interests have been thought of and tended to. They even anticipate the valuable chance to converse with one another, whether about little things or greater issues that requires a lot of work to determine.

You can have different sorts of communication with your mate and fortify the obligation of your marriage. On the off chance that you wish to know how to impart in a relationship really or how to open correspondence in a marriage, indeed, here are a few different ways you can do that:

a. Talk about everything.

One thing you can do to reinforce your marriage, keep serious areas of strength for it, shield your relationship from infidelity is to converse with one another consistently.

Discuss the significant things and the minor ordinary things. Imparting consistently will keep you and your life partner associated with one another.

It will likewise forestall both of you from looking for another person to impart to.

- Send your partner an "I love you" message or text around mid-afternoon just to tell them you give it a second thought.
- Share your triumphs and disappointments with your partner. For instance, call your partner when you get the advancement you've been pursuing for.
- Talk in the nights about world and nearby occasions. For instance, you could conclude that each night both of you will talk about governmental issues over supper.
- Try communicating via text, email, virtual entertainment, or video talk. It doesn't make any difference how you speak with one another, so be imaginative with it.

b. Listen to one another effectively.

Successful communication is one of the keys to making a marriage work. The better you and your partner communicate, the more straightforward it will be for you to determine struggle and keep your marriage working.

- Eliminate interruptions when you and your partner are having serious discussions. Remove the TV, hold on until the children are sleeping, and put your electronic gadgets on quiet or vibrate.
- Tell your partner you need an interruption free discussion. Express something like, "Hello, darling, would you see any problems with switching off the TV so we can discuss.

- □ Take a gander at your partner and request that your partner take a gander at you when all of you are examining things.
- □ Listen to what your partner is discussing allows your brain to float or contemplate what you will say accordingly. Attempt to ask as the need might arise to completely comprehend what they are talking about. Reflect back to them what you heard with the goal that they can affirm or explain.

c. Express your requirements.

One explanation individuals have illicit relationships is on the grounds that their requirements are not being met inside their ongoing relationship. You might go to somebody outside the union with satisfy your requirements in the event that you don't feel your partner is meeting them. You can shield your marriage from infidelity, however; assuming you ensure that you and your companion are both letting each other understand what you want from the marriage and from one another.

- □ Let your companion know when your requirements aren't being met in the relationship. For instance, you could need to say, "Honey, I know we're both occupied, however I want us to hang out."

- □ Offer your companion the chance to communicate their requirements. For example, tune in and focus assuming your mate lets you know that they need more communication or closeness. You can likewise hell back in occasionally to perceive how you're doing.

d. Set objectives together.

We have consistently defined objectives as a family and exclusively in four regions: profound, sporting, instructive, and monetary. I think we likely made our three children insane with this now and again; that being said, right up to the present day, they keep on laying out objectives and have a good time offering them to one another. As the maxim goes, "assuming you neglect to design, you intend to fall flat." Why not take a period this week to plunk down together and put forth a couple of practical objectives that you can start to pursue as a family?

DOS AND DONT TO IMPROVE YOUR COMMUNICATION IN MARRIAGE.

1. Attempt and Be Specific.

Whenever you wish to come to a meaningful conclusion, ensure you are explicit about it. Try not to skirt the real issue or discuss arbitrary things that are irrelevant. Abstain from summing up by offering expressions like "You generally say/do this". This may not settle the reason; all things being equal, you might wind up harming your companion.

2. Be Respectful.

Regardless of what sort of discussion you and your companion are having, it is vital to be deferential towards it. By being a decent audience, you show that you regard your partner. At the point when you tune in, your partner will do the equivalent when you need to say something.

3. Try not to Nag or Taunt.

Nobody likes getting singled out or annoyed, and similar turns out as expected for your mate. You can't continue to make your partner blameworthy or liable for his previous mishaps at whatever point you wish to come to a meaningful conclusion. Your partner needs to feel cherished and needed, and each time you insult your partner, it causes hurt and agony, yet it additionally influences your relationship. Likewise, never haul in relatives or companions when you have contentions.

4. Try not to Jump to Conclusions.

Try not to expect things or concoct your own accounts without having a word with your companion. You might blow up that your companion didn't get your call without understanding or allowing them an opportunity to make sense of why it worked out. Converse with your life partner about the thing is annoying you in regards to them and know reality behind their side of the story.

5. Have Regular Conversations.

Regardless of how occupied you are or the amount of work you possess to do, ensure you take out an opportunity in a day to have some significant discussion with your mate. On the off chance that you can't imagine anything to talk, get ridiculous or senseless and share a few loud chuckles with one another. It is vital to speak with your life partner consistently to keep the adoration streaming in the relationship.

6. No Blame Games.

Regardless of whether you are frantic in light of the fact that your life partner accomplished something wrong, beginning looking for someone else to take the blame isn't suggested. Perhaps your life partner might have had self-acknowledgment that a mix-up was committed and essential measures might have been taken to offer to set things straight. Be that as it may, regardless of whether there are no acknowledge, it is in every case better to put across a point unpretentiously and obligingly as opposed to raising a ruckus around town individual with every one of the faults.

7. Try not to Rely on Online Chatting.

At the point when you are away working or away from home, visiting through a mechanism of web based talking is helpful to a degree, however it can't substitute significant coordinated discussions or telephone discussions. Some of the time online methods of correspondence can prompt false impressions and disarrays and may strain blissful connections.

8. Don't Be Defensive.

In the event that your partner needs to draw out certain objections or issues against you, it is vital to pay attention to them eagerly without being protective about it. It is similarly difficult for your partner to acquire their own blemishes front of you. Ensure you tune in and go to viable lengths to tackle the issue as opposed to becoming cautious about the entire issue.

9. Be Tolerant.

We as a whole have various inclinations, likes or abhorrence, and the equivalent goes for two individuals who are married to one another. You might like watching cricket however your companion loves tennis; be thankful and open minded toward one another leisure activities, decisions and other such viewpoints as opposed to griping about them. Since when you become open, your partner will as well.

10. Express Positive Feelings.

The vast majority of us might discuss our concerns, strains, fears and other such gloomy sentiments more than we discuss good sentiments like love, sympathy, lowliness and so forth. Ensure you incorporate more good discussions, which would incorporate commending one another, showing adoration and care and other such good sentiments.

IMPORTANCE OF COMMUNICATION IN A MARRIAGE.

1. No Communication Implies No Interest.

In the event that you don't have the foggiest idea what's going on in your partner's life or what issues they might be managing, you will be unable to comprehend or relate. This would gradually prompt indifference for one another lives and subsequently, stressed connections; hence, having compelling communication is significant.

2. Better Understanding.

Couples who frequently talk, examine their lives or speak with each consistently not just have a superior comprehension with one another, however it likewise assists them with having a more grounded bond with one another. At the point when you comprehend your life partner and the circumstances they might manage, there would be lesser degree for misconception or vagueness.

3. Better Martial Satisfaction.

In the event that you have opened the entryways of viable correspondence with your companion, you are bound to encounter a blissful and quiet relationship. Better correspondence implies better fulfillment in a relationship in which you examine everything with one another and in this way lesser battles or fights.

4. Better Trust, Honesty and Respect.

Marriage is a two-way road; you can't simply continue anticipating all that without giving. However, on the off chance that you are straightforward with your mate and give and get positive criticism or offer different issues with complete genuineness, it assists in working with bettering confidence in a relationship.

5. Better Connection.

Correspondence is an approach to communicating your sentiments and feelings towards your life partner. We comprehend that it doesn't mean very much to communicate in words the adoration and fondness that you have for your life partner. Nonetheless, being expressive and vocal is one of the most incredible approaches to displaying your feelings towards your life partner, which would prompt a superior association.

2. KNOW YOUR LIMIT

Why Are Limits So Significant In Marriage?

Your relationship with your companion is perhaps of the main association throughout everyday life.

At the point when we set up the right limits, we keep our marriage in the right path and into a more healthy place for your marriage .

To defend your marriage, you really want to sort out what your limits are. In the event that you don't define limits for you and your partner, it will be difficult to tell when they have been crossed.

Limits are one of the main parts of sound connections. Limits characterize what your identity is and the amount you permit others to approach you.

There is a scarcely discernible difference between

defining limits and being childish, yet it comes from a position of affection, not fear.

Limits help to safeguard you, your relationship, and your marriage. For a union finding lasting success, the life partners should settle on what their own limits are and the way in which they will convey them to one another.

The following are four things you can do to set healthy boundaries:

1. Regard Your Own Sentiments, Feelings, and Necessities.

Socrates said, 'Know Yourself. 'At the point when you know your own restrictions, shortcomings, and weaknesses, you can make limits that work for you rather than against you. Limits are characterized by your own sentiments, assessments needs, and needs.

It means a lot to think often about yourself enough to perceive your limits and impart them plainly to your companion.

2. Regard your life partner's sentiments, conclusions, and necessities.

You should likewise be in line with your mate. You should comprehend that you can't anticipate that somebody should regard your limits in the event that you don't regard theirs. You can look into the limits of your marriage by focusing on how the other individual responds when they feel like their limits have been crossed.

Keep in mind, at this stage, we are defining limits so our life partner has a good sense of reassurance, safe, and regarded. Your limits ought to be about them, not you.

3. Figure out the 'why' behind your limits and focus on it.

For limits to work, you should know why you are defining the limit and be focused on it.

You should have a justification behind needing to define a particular limit. By knowing your 'why,' you can discuss your limits with conviction and veritable worry for other people. Ensure that the motivation behind your limit isn't something egotistical or out of fear

4. Impart Your Limits to Your Spouse.

At the point when you put down stopping points for you and afterward impart them obviously to your partner, you are safeguarding yourself from being harmed or exploited.

Believe through how you might want to be dealt with and what you might want to encounter in your marriage. This is a significant stage. It follows the 'do unto others as you would have them do unto you' rule. Never take part in an action that you don't believe your mate should take part in.

At the point when we remember this, we will make limits that safeguard our relationship since we have our life partner as a top priority.

Limits in marriage are fundamental for your relationship's well being. These limits ought to be made all together and not singularly forced by one companion. Laying out limits is a significant stage toward ensuring that you and your accomplice have a good sense of reassurance and blissful in your relationship.

Two Kinds of Marriage Limits

What sort of limits safeguards marriage? I think there are two essential sorts each couple ought to consider. There are external limits and internal limits. By a long shot the main (as I would see it) is the internal limits we have in our own hearts.

External Limits

These are guardrails we set up to screen our activities and conduct.

For instance, each couple ought to have limits about what is adequate and unsuitable virtual entertainment conduct. Outside limits are the actual responsibilities we make to our life partner to give them security, certainty, and trust that we won't cause anything to harm your marriage.

They characterize the boundaries of the relationship. They give a protected spot between two individuals who are seeing someone. There are a wide range of kinds of outside limits that can be utilized to accomplish this reason; Promises, pledges, arrangements, marriage responsibilities, and different standards are external limits that can be instituted to safeguard the marriage.

For instance, I have a companion who goes out to of the country regularly to convey lectures in gathering, classes. He has an incredible marriage and he comprehends the enticements of being away from his family, and the frailty his significant other could feel about his movements, so he generally goes with a male partner.

They put down this limit as a place of commitment. He realizes he could never hurt his better half by being faithless. Be that as it may, he sets up this defend for both of their security. It gives security in their relationship.

This is only one type of outside limits used to safeguard your relationship.

We prescribe taking time as a team to examine areas of instability, weakness, and likely risk. Then, at that point, build shields to set up that will consider you responsible and safeguard your marriage. They are outer limits since they include actual cutoff points we put on ourselves to watch our way of behaving.

The standard is, on the off chance that I don't place myself in a terrible circumstance, I won't succumb to the enticement. In the event that I'm in good company with another lady, I can't swindle. In any event, that is the idea. It has a few defects, however it makes a difference.

Internal Limits

Internal limits are those we set for ourselves to screen our contemplation's and words. These are the lines we attract on ourselves to remain in charge, and at times they're undetectable, similar to the limit between "going excessively far" and restraint.

We can be the cause all our own problems. We can make ourselves fall flat if we don't watch out. We can cause harm to ourselves and the one we love.

We need to give close consideration to our viewpoints, convictions, and self-talk. On the off chance that our inward discussion is excessively regrettable, there is potential for harming our marriage and in some cases ourselves all the while. We should call these heart limits, guides we set up in our own hearts and psyche to keep us sure and loyal. We would do well to lay out heart limits in our own life. One method for doing this is to defined limits on what we permit into our viewpoints. Monitoring what we watch on TV, what music we pay attention to, and what we open our eyes to on the web are exceedingly significant guards we can set up to safeguard our hearts.

This isn't about strict legalism. It is tied in with esteeming our marriage such a lot of we safeguard it by defending our considerations.

Our thought process about, we seek after. It's how we were planned. Our brains are like intensity looking for rockets. When they secure an objective (our thought process about), they move us toward that objective.

Assuming that you fill your contemplation's with negative things, your life will move toward those things. Assuming you fill your thought with positive things, you will move that way.

It's an unwritten, imperceptible law of nature.

Assuming you persistently have self-talk that grumbles about your marriage, you will ultimately Trust that internal exchange.

We frequently make statements we don't actually 'accept.' When we continually insist something, we ultimately acknowledge it and that conviction will rule our life.

That is the reason we really want to raise limits around our viewpoints, words, and convictions. They will eventually decide the course and outcome of our lives including our marriage.

Does Your Marriage Need Another Arrangement Of Limits?

To assist answer this inquiry and deal with your relationship limit needs, we should suggest a couple of conversation starters.

- □ Is it OK to hug another person of the opposite sex?

- □ Should a married person be alone (isolated) with the opposite sex?
- □ Should a husband defend his wife against insults from his immediate family?
- □ How important is parental approval in your relationship?
- □ What constitutes an unhealthy emotional connection with another person?

We get these inquiries habitually. A few inquiries are simpler to respond to than others. For instance, it is undesirable for a man to take one more lady to a confidential supper. It's unfortunate, however it is likewise perilous. You are getting yourself positioned for moral split the difference.

Different inquiries are not as simple to reply. These are what I call 'borderline inquiries.' We as a whole have this concealed line that decides when things are off-base - too far out. It's not only an ethical line. It is a moral and mental line. The borderline inquiries are responded to as per the bearing of your relationship. On the off chance that you are heading for your mate, you are in a safe zone. Assuming you are going 'away' from your mate, you are at serious risk.

Assuming your marriage is going off course, there are numerous things that are unfortunate that could somehow or another appear to be authentic.

Everything relies upon where you are and where you are going in your marriage.Strong Marriages Keep These Limits in Place

It isn't my plan to let you know what limits to lay out. That is something best finished as a couple. Limits (as I've attempted to clarify) are private. They ought to be worked around your requirements as a team. All things considered, the following are a couple of limits we consider good for all couples.

1. No One-On-One Private Meetings with the opposite Sex.

I utilize the term private which is as it should be. Your work circumstance might expect you to have an office meeting with a colleague or business partner of the other gender. Assuming that is the situation (and it is inescapable), ensure you stay responsible with your life partner.

It very well might be useful to talk about the gathering when with your mate. This sends the message you care about their sentiments and need to try not to cause them to feel unreliable.

2. . Keep Social Media Accounts Transparent.

While social media (Facebook, Instagram, TikTok) can serve a purpose, it can also be used to make someone feel uncomfortable. Make sure both your spouse has access to your social media accounts and are aware of any questionable posts.

Obsessing over social media is one of the negative habits deadly to your marriage.

- Give your spouse access to all of your social media accounts.
- Make sure that you and your spouse have access to each other's passwords for their email, text, and social media accounts.

- □ Be aware of the content you are posting on the internet that may make your spouse feel uncomfortable or insecure in any way shape or form.
- □ Do not post anything questionable on social media without first talking with your spouse about it to avoid creating any tensions between the two of you.
- □ No private social media accounts..

3. Set a schedule for Time Together.

There ought to be a limit (to safeguard it), and in addition to a thing on your plan for the day. Similarly as it is vital to be straightforward with your life partner, it is additionally critical to ensure they are feeling adored and appreciated also. You can do this by doing various things.

- □ Go On Dates
- □ Show Love
- □ Give Gifts and Roses (which are not connected with commemorations)
- □ Say "I Love You" 3-5 Times Each Day
- □ Know your life partner's way to express affection

4. Be Safe and Practical in All Decisions Made With Finances.

This is a frequently disregarded area of limits. However most couples live way outside their spending plan. It's not difficult to perceive what monetary difficulty means for marriage. Putting limits around our spending is fundamental.

It is hard to have a sound, blissful marriage without monetary dependability and having the option to take care of your bills. To have the option to cover your bills, you should be dependable with cash. The more you spend, the more you are in the red. To counterbalance this, you should make an equilibrium of saving as well as spending.

Monetary choices are vital and will extraordinarily influence your capacity to live serenely as well as the eventual fate of you and your family's monetary steadiness.

5. Keep Short Accounts with Each Other.

Keeping short records is the craft of talking about issues before they become huge issues. By practicing it regularly to examine issues consistently (everyday registration times) you try not to allow things to get made a huge deal about. The most effective way to try not to make huge issues not too far off is to discuss them. Discussing the issue brings issues to light and makes a culture of open exchange where everybody has a real sense of security raising worries.

Adhere to the 2-minute rule.

The 2-Minute Rule is a simple rule to adhere to that can assist you with keeping away from false impressions and relationship clashes. It essentially implies offer each other your unified consideration for two minutes. The two minutes don't have a clock connected to it either, so there is no strain to hurry through the discussion.

The following are a couple of things to recollect while utilizing the Brief Standards:

- You should have the option to offer each other your full consideration for two entire minutes without interruptions.
- At the point when you are finished with the two minutes, let your accomplice in on the time has come to continue on.
- Try not to interfere with one another.
- Your undivided focus implies no taking a gander at your telephone, PC or whatever else.

By adhering to the 2-Minute Guideline, you will assist with fortifying your relationship by permitting yourselves an opportunity to vent and discuss what is irritating you. Observe this guideline consistently and you will observe that you can stay away from a considerable lot of the enormous issues that emerge in connections and relationships overall.

3. CONFLICT RESOLUTION

A ton of harmful demonstrations happen in the marriage, particularly both profound and actual maltreatment. At the point when you get to hear what numerous companions, both male and female persevere, you begin contemplating whether getting married merits the work. Little marvel numerous relationships are at different degrees of deterioration: quiet home treatment, perniciousness, unfaithfulness, actual maltreatment, and partition; all causing divorce.

I chose to look at it to get our relationships against maltreatment, either profound or physical. I have come to understand that the main source of oppressive demonstrations, close to home or physical, is unfulfilled promises. A ton of married couples are not getting the normal fulfillment from the marriage setting, consequently prompting disappointment. The assumptions revolve around the purposes behind getting into the marriage: monetary security, friendship, sexual delight, and youngsters, among others. These vary from one individual to another, contingent upon individual character.

How to get your marriage against struggle?

Never increase current standards of expectations too high in the marriage. Comprehend that the best of human is as yet human. Consider disillusionment with the goal that you don't get disappointed, assuming it works out. Accept for something good, yet plan for just horrible. It's a functioning relationship treatment. You put the entire of your work into it, however have it as an arrangement B that failure is conceivable, and should be dealt with cautiously. It's difficult to accept, yet it is reality.

Compromise should be of highest need. Try not to allow clashes to putrefy. Stop it from ever really developing as fast as it comes. Clashes will undoubtedly occur in marriage since two people from two distinct foundations are meeting up to live as one, under one rooftop. Subsequently, you should not exclusively be proactive, yet deliberate, towards compromise. Allow it to be one of your early arrangements that the sun should not go down on your rage. Putrefying clashes breed profound and actual maltreatment.

a. Don’t provoke your spouse into abusive acts.

These can occur in the accompanying ways: what you say, do and imply. Every one of these incite married couples to get actual in the marriage. Like somebody said as of late, ladies are harshly toned, and can utilize it to incite their spouses, to high sky of actual maltreatment. For the spouses, don't incite your wives by unreliable way of behaving towards family prosperity and upkeep. It might draw out the most exceedingly awful of conduct from them. At the point when a spouse leaves his monetary responsibility to home liability, it becomes challenging for the wife not to adversely utilize her tongue. Allow us to help each other to remain serene in the marriage.

b. Don't threaten your spouse..

It conveys message of frailty in the marriage. The person will become or feel unstable in the marriage, in this manner begins getting into profound gloom and becoming delicate on issues. This is much of the time the place where actual maltreatment becomes inescapable. As of now you might be wrongly incited.

Be delicate to the profound condition of your companion.Events of loss of occupations, business disappointment, ought to draw in concern and thoughtful comprehension and backing from the life partner. It's not in such conditions that a mate becomes irrational in setting expectations for the bothered accomplice.

Think about the winding impacts of your struggles on your partner.

This is a piece of the outcomes treatment. Kids, parents in law, companions, organizations, all endure when a marriage is in emergency. Thus, don't be self centered in your conjugal choices. Put others into thought before you cause trouble in your marriage. Try not to simply think about your misfortunes in taking choices; count the misfortunes of other people who are involved with you and your companion.

At the point when we put every one of these into thought, the occurrence of maltreatment in the marriage setting will be in the most reduced ebb, while possibly not completely wiped out, turning into the exemption, as opposed to the standard.

c. Be cautious who you tell about conflict.

You might be enticed to tirade or vent to your companions about the issues happening in your marriage, yet this isn't generally smart. The companion that you are venting to may attempt to involve the data as a method for enticing you (or your mate) with an undertaking. Rather than telling others the close insights regarding your relationship, shield your marriage from infidelity by conversing with your companion about your issues first. Going to another person to vent about your marriage might open the entryway for enticement. For instance, you might get going conversing with a companion about your marriage and afterward wind up succumbing to your companion just in light of the fact that you are irate with your mate.

Consider whether you would need your life partner offering your conjugal issues to their companions. In some cases conversing with an expert, similar to a marriage mentor can fortify your marriage as a result of the objectivity they bring to the circumstance and critical thinking strategies they can impart to you and your companion.

A decent guideline is to just discuss your union with parties that have been settled upon by the two sides.

d. Fight fair.

One thing that can bring on some issues in a marriage is when mates assault each other during struggle as opposed to settling the genuine issue. At the point when this happens it can make more concerning issues that open the entryway for infidelity. You can safeguard your marriage from breaking in the event that you ensure that you are taking care of the contentions in your marriage in a developed way.

Try not to call each other names. For instance, calling your significant other 'inept' or 'lethargic' in light of the fact that you believe he should do a few home fixes is definitely not an effective method for tending to struggle. Try not to express things to hurt your companion purposefully. For example, raising the reality your better half lost her employment when you realize it annoys her. Stick to resolving the issue.

e. Learn to apologize and to forgive.

Clutching outrage, feelings of spite, and disdain can destroy any marriage - even without an issue. At the point when you misunderstand followed through with something, be grown-up enough to apologize. Furthermore, as the need should arise, be grown-up enough to pardon. Remember that pardoning doesn't be guaranteed to imply that full trust is reestablished. That part frequently takes more time. Pardoning is a decision - trust is something that takes work. Nonetheless, the capacity to say you are heartbroken and to pardon might be quite possibly of the main thing you can do to shield your marriage from breaking.

Pardoning isn't imagining that something didn't occur or that it didn't do any harm. It's anything but a programmed remedy for the heart, since transgression has results that wait. Pardoning is certainly not a characteristic human reaction, however nor is it inconceivable. Pardoning is a decision to liberate the other party from the obligation or offense that they have committed against you. It is a disposition of relinquishing disdain and my entitlement to settle the score, and an activity should be communicated by word and deed.

At the point when you have effectively harmed or dishearten your life partner, then, at that point, let them know you are sorry straightaway. You could have a go at saying, "Honey, Please accept my apologies for what I did. I realize that I hurt you and I never implied for that to occur. Can you at any point pardon me?"

Let your companion know that you excuse them assuming they misunderstand followed through with something. In some cases you need to do this regardless of whether they haven't apologized. For example, you could say, "Darling, I was upset and what you did hurt me. However, I do accept your apology and forgive you, though.

f. Seek counseling.

There might be some of the time in your marriage that speaking with one another, being personal, and addressing struggle aren't sufficient to safeguard your marriage from breaking. You might have irritating issues, significant struggle, or need an alternate point of view on the best way to safeguard your marriage. Looking for mentoring from a family or marriage specialist can furnish you and your companion with the help and methodologies you want to help forestall both of you from committing infidelity.

- Try not to put off looking for marriage mentoring all things considered. Standing by too lengthy can make it harder to manage the issues. You can look for marriage mentoring in any event, for little issues in your relationship to assist with fighting off serious issues.
- □ Think about looking for directing from your strict chief in the event that all of you are dynamic in a strict local area.

- □ Investigate marriage support bunches that can give you and your life partner a method for looking for help.
- □ Converse with a marriage mentor or comparative expert to resolve difficult issues in your relationship.

g. Accept reality.

Now and again, there is a way to safeguard your marriage from breaking. It is possible that you or your companion are not dedicated to the relationship, or dislike commitment overall. Assuming you have given your very best for shield your marriage from breaking yet at the same time feel or realize that an issue is happening, you want to embrace the truth and choose how to address it.

Assuming you or your life partner has committed infidelity before, it might require additional work on both of your parts to safeguard the marriage from infidelity later on.

Recall that it takes two individuals to make a marriage work. You need to just let it out and address it if both of you're not dedicated to keep the marriage liberated from undertakings.

h. Be purposeful in resolving conflict

We fly off the handle when we feel that our freedoms have been abused, our assumptions have not been met, or our mate has harmed us here and there. At the point when this occurs, we normally answer in one of two ways: we stuff it (assimilate it) or blow it (externalize it). Anyway we respond, unsettled struggle prompts disconnection from one another. Walls are assembled, step by step, inactively or forcefully. We have a choice between bitterness and tension on the one hand, and forgiveness and freedom on the other.

4. DATE YOUR SPOUSE

Since you and your life partner are married doesn't mean going on ordinary dates together ought to stop. Many couples observe that they are less happy with their marriage when they don't invest purposeful energy with their life partner. It is exceptionally considered normal to stall out in the standard cycle and quit giving opportunity to enjoy with your life partner. Perhaps you and your life partner have encountered the bluntness of ordinary everyday practice. Therefore dating, regardless of whether you're married, means a lot to rehearse. Dating is urgent to keep your marriage energizing and to light the flash both of you have consistently.

Why is it Important to Date Your Spouse?

Dating Your Companion Can Be Surprisingly Significant. A few couples feel that setting aside a few minutes for dates is insignificant. All things considered, you see your life partner at home consistently and get a lot of them. In all actuality, when couples keep on dating subsequent to getting married, they foster better relational abilities, are generally a lot more joyful and more dedicated to one another, and will quite often have lower separate from rates. At the point when you commit one night seven days, each and every other week, or even once a month to date evenings, you will feel like you began dating your companion once more. You will feel considerably more associated with them than previously. Furthermore, you have something to anticipate all through your bustling week. Here are a portion of the reasons it is so critical to work on eating while you're married:

1. **To Keep the Spark Alive.**

At the point when you feel like you and your mate is beginning to date once more, it tends to very energize. In this manner, the heartfelt flash among you will start to get a lot more splendid. You will begin getting butterflies back in your stomach. Your companion might look into you, and you can find out about them. It will fortify your relationship and cause it to feel like another involvement in your exceptional individual. Whether you have been married for a couple of years or married for a really long time, getting some margin to date and your life partner is certainly not an exercise in futility. Carving out opportunity to go out to supper or see a film with your mate can appear to be a torment. You are logical exceptionally occupied with work, school, children, and all the other things that might be requesting your time. Getting some margin to go out on the town can feel like an additional obligation regarding your week after week plan for the day. Truly, overlooking the requirement for putting time to the side to foster your marriage is one of the most well-known purposes behind low fulfillment levels in marriage. When you are on the date, you might feel better to disregard your different obligations. At the point when you plan an opportunity to have a great time, one-on-one time with your companion, you will prize date evenings and the flash they take back to your marriage.

2. To Have a Deep Friendship to Fall Back On..

Not exclusively will dating your mate reignite the fire, yet additionally it will reinforce your kinship. It means a lot to realize that you and your companion are something other than a wedded couple. You are a unit that cooperates. You ought to have a significant companionship with your life partner as it can prompt higher marriage fulfillment and a lower opportunity of separation.

At the point when you and your life partner experience struggle, having a profound and significant fellowship with your companion to return to makes dealing with the contention a lot more straightforward. Going on dates in your marriage can help you and your mate fosters your fellowship. As you hang out, you will probably find you and your companion interface considerably more than you did previously. You can assist with developing your relationship and make numerous cheerful recollections together. Each marriage deals with issues, so when challenges go crazy, having these extraordinary recollections can assist you with feeling more propelled to make up with your companion.

3. To Slow Down and Make Time for Each Other.

Creating night out a propensity can help you and your life partner makes sure to set aside a few minutes for one another. Dialing back and enjoying a little while hours with your companion can make life considerably more agreeable. Individuals will more often than not be two times as cheerful while investing energy with their mates. In this way, make an honest effort to set aside a few minutes for your accomplice, regardless of how occupied your timetable is.

While pushing through your morning and evening time schedules, attempt to dial back and make a date out of it. In the mornings, rather than simply passing by one another, take a stab at getting to know each other. Attempt to have breakfast together or have some espresso together. Around evening time, do likewise and partake in supper together and be purposeful while conversing with one another. In this day and age, setting aside a few minutes for somebody when you have a furious timetable is extremely significant. Being deliberate when both of you hang out will make your relationship a lot more grounded and charming. On the off chance that you believe you and your life partner haven't been setting aside a few minutes for one another, take a stab at making going on dates a customary event.

HOW TO DATE YOUR SPOUSE

a. Show your spouse that you care

You can assist with shielding your marriage from infidelity assuming you put forth certain that you are making an attempt to show your mate that you love them. Be certain that you contemplate what is important to "them", not you. Your life partner might believe you should take a task off their plan for the day, not get them a gift, or the other way around. It doesn't need to be anything large or major, however getting some margin to tell your mate you care can hold you and them back from wandering. It's likewise an approach to advising yourself that you care about your companion.

- Leave your mate a little note in the restroom or the kitchen that says "I love you".

- Accomplish something uniquely amazing for your companion just to show them that you care about. For instance, give your better half a back rub when she returns home.
- Make a rundown of the relative multitude of reasons you love your mate and everything you like about them. Mail the rundown to their work or give it to them one day.

b. Schedule dates.

Despite the fact that you are married, you can in any case (and ought to in any case) set up dates with one another. Going out together permits you to invest energy with one another beyond the house. Getting to know each other will likewise keep the 'flash' and energy in your marriage.

Plan a standard night out with your life partner. For instance, each and every other Friday night could be night out on the town for both of you. Plan a sitter in the event that you have children. Try not to simply head off to some place together. Get some margin to put on an exceptional outfit, dress yourself up a little, and cause it to feel like a date.

As thought up as it might feel to plan a repetitive night out, this may be the best way to make it conceivable! Having something on your timetable (and adhering to your timetable!) will make night out bound to occur. This doesn't need to be a week by week event (however it tends to be) and it doesn't imply that you can't have unconstrained date evenings (you thoroughly ought to) it's an approach to carving out opportunity to be together. Night out needn't bother with to be some intricate difficulty (regardless of whether it is set apart on the schedule), it simply should be a couple of hours or a night put away to develop closeness in your relationship. Assuming you are threatened by putting something on your schedule or feel like this comes down on night out, you can assign the arranging part to various applications that can assist you with tracking down fun exercises to do in your space. Or on the other hand you can involve this as a potential chance to find new leisure activities to do together! Figure out how to make dating tomfoolery and something to anticipate by writing in your schedule and making it into an exceptional time together.

Get sentiment updates, fun night out thoughts and intelligent tests.

c. Do Something Both of You Appreciate

To begin, have a go at doing something you both appreciate to help both of you bond over a common interest. In the event that you or your mate is reluctant about routinely dedicating time to dates, this can be a major inspiration. Your dates ought to be invigorating for both of you, so doing a movement you both appreciate is an extraordinary method for starting off dating while you're married. Whether that is a climbing, trekking, going to satire shows, shopping, going out to eat, or heading out to the motion pictures, do a movement with your mate. You could likewise attempt to go on a street outing to a town neither of you has at any point been to.

Along these lines, you can make an entire day of your unique date with your mate.

On the off chance that you and your mate are where you have barely any familiarity with one another any longer, just sit back and relax. Attempt to plunk down with your companion and ask them what they appreciate doing in their available energy. From that point, conceptualize thoughts for what both of you will partake in doing together. You and your mate probably have no less than one normal interest, so attempt to begin a night out with that movement.

d. Throwback to the start of your relationship

On the off chance that you're battling to come up with thoughts for night out, or can't become excited up for evaluating your partner action, consider doing the sorts of things you did together toward the start of your relationship. Doing exercises that at first united you as a team can assist you with keeping up with the sentiments you had when you were in the tomfoolery and lighthearted romance stage in your marriage stage.

e. Prioritize intimacy

Set aside a few minutes for closeness. Perhaps of everything thing you can manage to help a solid marriage and forestall infidelity is to ensure you are hanging out. There are loads of ways you can get physically involved with your companion. Consider ways that you can spend together, appreciating each other's conversation and presence.

If discussing intimacy is an area of anxiety or dread for you, consult a professional to discuss it. Not discussing these concerns is one of the fastest ways to deteriorate a marriage.

If you need to, then schedule a night for intimacy. It might be as simple as a few hours of cuddling or even a plan for a romantic sexual evening.

Take the time to do things like hug, kiss, hold hands, and hold each other. Try to do these things on a regular basis.

Dating should be fun. Going on dates can be a great way to blow off steam after a busy couple of days and try something new with your partner. But it's also important that you work to incorporate intimacy into your date nights. After all, you are romantic partners! Yes, this does mean sex. And, yes, sex is important, but when we talk about intimacy we also mean romantic and physical intimacy.

Also, focusing on sex and planning time for it assuming that is vital in your bustling timetable, or simply something that you like to do), plan heartfelt time together. Heartfelt time can be a decent night out, preparing an extravagant feast at home, going on a heartfelt outing together or even going on a night walk, interruption free so you can absorb each other's organization. Viewing ways as close with each other will work on your association, fortify your bond, and furthermore further develop you sexual coexistence by expanding your appreciation for your accomplice.

a. Table your standard ideas

At the point when you truly do carve out the opportunity to go out on the town, and be cozy, recognizing the date from a customary activity can be significant. You maintain that the date should feel extraordinary partially (not constantly, but rather most certainly a portion of the time), so try not to discuss the things you typically examine (otherwise known as don't discuss work or what you will get from the supermarket later in the week). Find opportunity to registration with your accomplice genuinely. Discuss your inclinations, things you maintain that should do together or think back about bygone eras! Dating is tied in with valuing your time together and talking about new, fascinating things! Assuming that you are battling to discuss new things, you and your accomplice can, think about looking into night out ice breakers (handily found on the web or even in relationship books). In fact, this sounds a little cheesy.... Yet, assuming you and your accomplice are available to it, ice breakers can assist with starting fascinating discussions about new points!

b. Consider your love languages

Plan a date in view of your ways to express affection. Main avenues for affection are one of the freshest and trendiest types of relationship brain research. The reasoning is that each individual has a favored method for giving adoration and a favored method for getting love, which might possibly coordinate with their accomplices. Main avenues for affection are separated into five classifications: uplifting statements, acts of service, getting gifts, quality time and physical touch. Every individual has a favored way to express affection, or a couple of favored ways to express affection that direct their way of behaving and assumptions in a relationship. When you sort out what your main avenues for affection are, plan a date that is reciprocal to these inclinations! Do you both incline toward quality time? Do an action together! Does one individual like gifts? Plan a date around presents! Get imaginative with your date thoughts and help show and get love in your favored ways.

c. Take a day off

This is certainly not a very reasonable tip for everybody, except contingent upon the sort of work you do and whether you can go home for the day or exchange movements or what have you, it can be enjoyable to require investment away from work to focus on your relationship. In the rushing about of life, it can be difficult to require the vital investment to develop your association with your accomplice. Once in a while requiring only one day off and spending that together can have a significant effect regarding your association. On the off chance that this is absurd, yet you actually feel like work is impeding night out/your association with your accomplice consider ways of keeping your work and home life independent. Could you at any point leave the workplace prior? Might you at any point begin your day after the fact with the goal that you have additional time together in the first part of the day? Could you at any point stay away from extra time so you can focus on your experience with your accomplice? Your occupation really should doesn't detract from investing energy and exertion towards building a more grounded bond with your accomplice.

5. BUILDING TRUST

Each great relationship is based upon trust. We as a whole realize that a marriage without trust resembles a vehicle without gas, it in all likelihood won't run. Knowing how to recapture trust and, surprisingly, even better, keep up with it in any case is fundamental to making a flourishing marriage. That is particularly evident with regards to marriage.

You decided to share EVERYTHING to the individual you love the most, so a work from the two companions to respect this commitment is essential to the progress of your relationship.

Little, small “white lies”, omissions, or even hiding the truth to avoid hurting our loved one, though not always motivated by wrong principles, can be very damaging to trust..

Work on many of the things of life together so that there’s not even room for the temptation of secrets or lies.

Assuming you fear giving criticism or counsel since you figure it might hurt your companion, learn savvy ways of saying it, yet don't hush up about it in the event that it should be said.

Promise to be just about as straightforward and fair as could really be expected.

Nobody is perfect, but everyone can have good communication, humility, and a willingness to work with their spouse.

But did you ever consider that there are different kinds of trust and we need all 4 of them to make our relationship work?

Even though we are all familiar with wedding vows, to love honor and cherish, there are promises that we might never say out loud that are the foundation for a marriage to last and, more importantly, be happy. Safety, Faithfulness, Commitment and Reliability are 4 pillars of trust each marriage needs. If any of these is feeling the loss of, the rooftop begins caving in and the relationship begins to break down.

1. Safety

Relationships flourish when the two accomplices have a solid sense of reassurance and security.

You need to believe that your accomplice won't hurt you, to have the option to contact them when you really want assistance, to be vulnerable and share your existence with them as well as your deepest desires.

Whether it's physical or verbal - any sort of dismissal works on trust.

One form of rejection that you may not be aware of, is the all too common “nagging.” If you nag, you are saying, “I don’t trust you will do your part.”

A loving reminder is okay. “Nagging” is a sign that there is a trust issue that hasn’t been addressed and a deeper conversation is called for. The next time you hear it or feel tempted to do it – pause and ask, “What is really needed here?”

That goes two different ways - we likewise need to keep our responsibilities once we make them. More on unwavering quality later here.

2. faithfulness

One more sort of trust that relationships need is faithfulness. That does without saying right? Without sexual loyalty we can't foster any of different sorts of trust.

Actual loyalty and profound constancy remain closely connected, so imparting your mysteries to your mate is really a method for building close to home unwavering in your marriage.

Trust is underlying tiny minutes in which one individual moves in the direction of their accomplice when they're out of luck. At the point when our accomplice answers emphatically, by "being there" as far as we might be concerned, that forms trust." When we are "there" for one another again and again, we can likewise start to trust each other even with outrage or upset.

Returning to that sense of safety - we as a whole need to realize that individual will be there in any event, when something is turning out badly.

Having a standard procedure that says, "its OK to be furious, I am staying put," is a vital structure block to trust and like profound concrete in your relationship.

Sexual faithfulness in marriage incorporates something other than our bodies. It likewise incorporates our eyes, brain, heart, and soul. At the point when we give our brains to sexual dreams about someone else, we penance sexual unwavering to our life partner. At the point when we offer snapshots of profound affections to another, we penance sexual steadfastness to our mate.

Watch your sexuality everyday and dedicate it altogether to your companion. Sexual loyalty requires self-control and an attention to the results. Decline to place anything before your eyes, body, or heart that would think twice about loyalty.

3. Commitment

It's likewise important that the two accomplices proclaim their marriage as a first concern both in hanging out and in carrying the commitments of day to day life.

To begin with, by concentrating intensely on your relationship, that shows the other individual they make a difference to you. You are placing them above different things. It likewise assists work with trusting in light of the fact that you are making proof that you are solid, that you can be relied on and trusted. The capacity to depend in one another as a group is fundamental to support trust over the long haul.

4. Reliability

As may be obvious, every support point fabricates and upholds the other. Reliability is the glue that keeps every one of the support points intact as - believing you will do what you say you will do is fundamental for security, steadfastness and responsibility.

Knowing the elements of what makes trust can likewise assist you with checking whether there is a region in your marriage where you are not feeling or communicating trust. This way you can re-construct that support point before it separates.

Perhaps of everything thing you can manage in your union with construct trust is make snapshots of well being, close to home security where your accomplice feels like they can associate with you and show weakness regardless be heard and cherished.

Genuineness and trust become the establishment for everything in a fruitful marriage. Yet, not at all like the vast majority of different basics on this rundown, trust takes time. You can become magnanimous, committed, or patient in a second, however trust generally takes time. Trust is just worked after weeks, months, and long periods of being who you say you are and doing what you say you'll do. It requires investment, so begin now — and assuming you want to modify trust in your relationship, you'll have to work considerably more enthusiastically.

6. APPRECIATING AND VALUING YOUR SPOUSE.

Successful relationships tend to have similar characteristics and qualities. These can vary in how they present, but generally speaking, couples who engage in joyful and positive connections share several elements.

Appreciating your spouse is a binding factor in relationships. Showing your spouse you appreciate and value them can be challenging; every person likes to receive affection and appreciation differently.

This is the person you have committed your life to, which shows you love them every day.

Sure, they have their moments as we all do, but this is the person who truly is the love of your life—and so you want to show your love and appreciation, and just how important they are to you.

This doesn't need to be anything elaborate or expensive, for sometimes the smallest tokens can help to show appreciation in a really big way. It's all about thinking through what they like, what makes them happy, and what will help them to feel important and loved when all is said and done.

Take a look at the following elements of a connected and positive relationship, then look at your own to evaluate whether or not these are present.

1. Prioritize

Life is frequently occupied. We frequently become mixed up in the mix between work, school, exercises and interests, and family obligations. This can make it considerably more testing to see and address the issues or needs of your companion. Valuing your mate is the last thing to enter your thoughts.

No movement or obligation ought to be a higher priority than the individual you love. At the point when your day to day routine becomes furious, require a couple of moments to focus on your day or week.

Have you included opportunity to address the requirements of your companion? It is fundamental to make the individual who is your accomplice your priority - keeping your main concerns in order is significant! Try not to let any person or thing hinder setting aside a few minutes for your mate and giving appreciation.

2. Quality time

Talking about time, quality time is fundamental for keeping any relationship solid. There is no space to develop, change, and advance together without it. The time put away with expectation is generally significant. You are telling your companion that in addition to the fact that they are significant, that you esteem each and every second spent close by. Make it a point to put the phone down, disconnect from social media, and partake in the time while valuing your life partner.

3. Vocal Gratitude

It isn't sufficient to say "much obliged" at times. At the point when your companion has accomplished something kind or made a special effort to make the busyness of life a smidgen bit easier, set aside some margin to begin valuing your mate and genuinely offer thanks. Value your better half or spouse with a no limits approach. Sending appreciation statements or connections statements to a your life partner is great to get started.

Searching for ways of valuing your better half? Value them for their thoughtful gestures and mindfulness, and in particular, say thanks to them in both public and private. Quotes valuing your accomplice can assist you with looking for motivation for inventive ways of saying thanks to your cooperate with an adoration note well tucked alongside a gift.

However, it need not be a costly gift. Likewise, saying thanks to your significant other or spouse ought not be an errand yet ought to easily fall into place. Express gratitude toward them for being your mainstay of solidarity, for assisting you in any little and large ways they with doing.

Searching for appreciation thoughts that don't cost? Indeed, there are other extremely valuable ways of valuing your companion. You should simply, plunk down and diary down every possible "I value my partner because" reflect the amount you esteem your relationship and won't cost a dime!

While valuing your companion, be explicit about what you appreciate: "Thank you for cutting while I was working today. I feared doing that when I returned home, so it was a wonderful little treat when it was finished!" Thank them for what they do as well as for what their identity is: "Thank you for being so ready to listen when I got back home from a terrible day at work today. It caused me to feel significant and significant.

4. Assistance with return

You ought to do likewise for your accomplice. Carve out opportunity to get some information about their day and really tune in, regardless of whether it isn't appealing. Be steady when your accomplice is harming - recollect, you are their safe place. Accomplish something kind without looking for activity consequently; unselfish thoughtful gestures can be the most incredibly contacting and make a remarkable feeling of association between spouse, showing your eagerness toward valuing your mate.

5. Public affirmation

Appreciation and consideration can exceptionally convey love and friendship, for example, appreciating your life partner in private. Nonetheless, public affirmation of accomplishments or demonstrations of administration can make an entirely different feeling of appreciation. A spouse who straightforwardly perceives and commends their life partner before others says something with witnesses, frequently reinforcing the earnestness of gratefulness.

It frequently implies more to the beneficiary assuming the assertion is made unafraid of who might tune in. Spouse appreciation, some of the time verging on even unfit commendation, is everything necessary to implant power and strength in your relationship.

6. "Before any other person"

Put your accomplice first. Esteem your significant other or spouse. Nothing talks about appreciation or worth more than treating the individual you love as though they are indispensable. The spouse who feels appreciated and valued by the person they have chosen to partner with is likely to engage in more physical intimacy and openness in communication. It is sometimes not enough to “invite” them to participate in a shared activity.

Sometimes it requires going beyond your usual range of familiarity or putting the interests of your companion in front of your own. Kindly focus on what they appreciate and who they like being near. Making a special effort to place your life partner first in everything can have quite a few advantages with minimal risk.

7.Send them a message to show them your affection and appreciation

How to appreciate someone you love without burning a hole in your pocket? Send them an adoration filled message. Valuing somebody you love doesn't get more straightforward than this. There's nothing better compared to an unexpected text around mid-afternoon to make you grin.

To show appreciation in connections to your first love, then send them a quick message in a bustling business day, basically to tell them you're considering them and that you love them. Phrases like, "I love you and value you," or a straightforward joke like, "I value you," will do wonders. It's startling, and it's basic, yet those couple of words can mean to such an extent.

You can likewise look for adoration appreciation cites or valuing your accomplice quotes on the web and offer them with them to surprise them. You will feel thrilled as you discover them radiating when they see you later on — once more, the easily overlooked details mean so much with regards to showing appreciation in connections!

8. Do something for them for no reason at all

You needn't bother with a unique event to accomplish something decent for them.

It likewise needn't bother with to be anything extravagant, for it tends to be basically as straightforward as a card or giving them a back rub.

The significant part here is to get some down time to benefit them, for not a glaringly obvious explanation by any means, and without any hidden obligations.

Heartfelt signals by your accomplice cause you to feel wanted

You're not doing this to get anything yourself, yet rather to assist them with feeling cherished in a basic yet significant manner.

The easily overlooked details will assist with putting a grin all over, and they will feel significant for being valued seeing someone, due to these little badge of appreciation in connections.

9. Cook their number one feast

One of the ways of showing appreciation in a relationship is by cooking for your better half. What a straightforward plan to see the value in adoration! Cook their favorite supper so they are shocked when they return home and it's hanging tight for them. This is most certainly one of the most mind-blowing ways of showing appreciation for your partner.

Prepare their lunch for them one day out of nowhere, or even try at astounding them with breakfast in bed. The way to the heart is through the stomach — and making them a most loved dinner makes certain to assist them with feeling appreciated and feed their body and soul. Appreciation in connections comes from easily overlooked details, and cooking their favorite dish is only one method for getting it done.

10. Give them a day off from responsibilities

We as a whole become involved with everything we need to do, and at times allowing them a vacation day to unwind can make all the difference.

Nothing can work better compared to this - saving them from their obligations, regardless of whether it is only for a solitary day, it is one of the most outstanding ways of showing appreciation in connections that mean such a huge amount to you. Let them know that it's their day to unwind, and you assume control over their obligations around the house.

Do the shopping for food, clean the house, cut the grass, or accomplish something with the goal that they don't need to.

Permit them an opportunity to stay in bed and unwind and show them that you are doing this since you value all that they accomplish for you.

It's one day, and however it implies more work for you, it will go far in assisting them with feeling really appreciated.

Telling somebody you value them doesn't need your words or gifts. Nice thoughts like the one referenced here can say a lot of the amount they mean to you and that they are valued for what their identity is.

11. Pamper them and set the tone for a day of love

Spoil them and set the vibe for a day of adoration and consideration. Nothing can assist an individual with feeling valued very like a day of spoiling! On the off chance that you are tight on reserves, set up a spa day at home. Ladies just love to get spoiled, and this is one of the most amazing ways of showing appreciation.

On the off chance that you value your lady, simply spoil them a great deal. That is the stunt!

Draw them a shower, set up candles, make them an extraordinary lunch, and give them a back rub. Everybody likes to be dealt with sometimes, and this goes far in giving them an opportunity to loosen up and consider the amount they mean to you simultaneously.

12. Show affection

Showing appreciation in a relationship goes a long way in cementing your love bond. As mentioned earlier, appreciating your girlfriend or partner requires no words or gifts.

Just hold onto them in that hug a little longer. Kiss a little deeper, and look them in the eyes with the affection that you have. Sometimes you do have to actually show that appreciation through affection and love.

And, this is one of the perfect answers to the question, how to appreciate your lover.

When you can look them in the eyes and make physical intimacy and that connection a true priority, then you are telling them all that they need to know.

Though life gets busy, working to keep that bond and physical connection strong will ensure that they know how you feel and show it to them without speaking any words at all.

It is crucial to appreciate those who love you and stand by you through thick and thin to weather the storms together. So, learn how to show appreciation without saying anything.

13. Talk to them, remind them why you love them

On how to show appreciation to your partner, the best tip is to appreciate your loved ones and help them by supporting them. Being there for somebody that you love is often one of the best ways to show appreciation in relationships.

Help them through something or just listen to them when they need you. Though it's always nice to show appreciation to the love of your life in unique ways, it can also be about getting back to basics when it comes to showing love and appreciation.

Men, appreciate your woman verbally as much as you can, for they love hearing about it. Women, don't just get charmed by this, do reciprocate.

So, how to tell someone how much you appreciate them? Remind them why you love them, show them that you are there for them, and help to support them when they need a little lift.

When somebody knows that they can count on you, then it's the ultimate compliment, and it helps to build somebody up when they need it. A little gesture can go a long way, and the appreciation will always be reciprocated too!

Reinforce your relationship with appreciation

For each relationship, appreciation is one the very utmost mantras.

A relationship runs on endeavors and appreciation. When you start understanding your mate's commitment to your life and ensure that you recognize them and value them, your relationship certain to thrive.

The strategies explained above are not an exhaustive list of ways to show your spouse how much you appreciate and love them, they are simple and almost immediately effective for appreciating your spouse. Do not be afraid to go out of your way to show your partner they come first. Try to be consistent with using one or two of these approaches, and you may soon find yourself reaping the many benefits of selflessness in a relationship.

The strategies explained above are not an exhaustive list of ways to show your spouse how much you appreciate and love them, they are simple and almost immediately effective for appreciating your spouse. Do not be afraid to go out of your way to show your partner they come first. Try to be consistent with using one or two of these approaches, and you may soon find yourself reaping the many benefits of selflessness in a relationship.

7. BE COMMITED

A deeper — and essential, if you want your marriage to last — level of commitment is needed. It's a commitment to be willing to do whatever it takes to make the marriage work, and that means there are going to be many times when you're just not going to get your way. And you're going to have to be OK with it, they say.

"It's not difficult to be focused on your relationship while it's working out positively. As a relationship changes, nonetheless, shouldn't you say eventually something like, 'I'm focused on this relationship, however it's not going quite well — I want to have some determination, make a few forfeits and make the strides I really want to take to keep this relationship pushing ahead. It's not only that I like the relationship, which is valid, yet that I will move forward and find dynamic ways to keep up with this relationship, regardless of whether getting everything I could possibly want in specific areas implies I'm not going'? This is the other sort of commitment: the contrast between 'I like this relationship and I'm focused on it' and 'I'm focused on taking the necessary steps to make this relationship work.'

At its core, love is a decision to be committed to another person. It is far more than a fleeting emotion as portrayed on television, the big screen, and romance novels. Feelings come and go, however a genuine choice to be committed endures everlastingly — and that characterizes sound relationships.

Marriage is a choice to be committed through the ups and the downs, the great and the terrible. At the point when things are working out in a good way, commitment is simple. However, genuine affection is shown by staying committed even through the preliminaries of life.

Commitment is only individuals' conviction to remain together. It is part of the relationship that provides well being and security, so couples can transparently offer their viewpoints, sentiments, and wants. Commitment is required in a wide range of connections. However, by and large, it’s romantic relationships that require more commitment than friendships.

Commitment isn't a legal contract. Be that as it may, when you mark yourself as a team, there is a common and unwritten figuring out between the partners.

The specific clauses of this understanding are rarely unequivocally expressed. In any case, as a piece of a serious relationship, it is normal that both the accomplices love one another, be steadfast, and stand by one another in difficult stretches.

For what reason is commitment significant in a marriage?

At the point when you start with a relationship, you could find it trying to commit at the commencement. In spite of being enamored, it requires investment to construct trust and reinforce the bonding.

Yet, in the event that you are anticipating a satisfying and enduring relationship, commitment is an important fixing to keep the spark alive.

Commitment is necessary for each partner to have a sense of security.

Having a solid sense of reassurance in a relationship cultivates love, confidence, and devotion. It gives boldness to the two partners to dream and plan things together for a long time to come.

Commitment doesn’t mean killing your freedom or losing your individuality. In fact, when you are in a relationship, commitment helps you become resilient during challenging times.

It is soothing to realize that you have each other's back during the difficult stretches. Thus, commitment is similarly essentially as significant as adoration and enthusiasm in a relationship. Commitment most likely has more to do with making relationships work than anything save normal qualities. It's not just about saying marriage promises or having a piece of paper that says "marriage permit". Commitment is significant on the grounds that we act distinctively when we realize that our prospects are integrated. You might stay away from a thorny discussion in the event that you realize the other partner won't be around for eternity. You may move on to another love if your current one shows no more care or simply starts to treat you the wrong way.

Commitment implies you've vowed to remain and work it through, today as well as until the end of time.

Commitment is a decision to surrender decisions. it really brings incredible opportunity and profundity. No longer does the serious individual need to weigh which individual or lifestyle will give more joy. When committed, all one's energy goes into genuinely committing to this relationship work.

The two significant phases of commitment are making the initial commitment and keeping the commitment.

1. Making the initial commitment

How commitment impacts marital happiness has centered on making the initial commitment. I have compared couples who cohabit before marriage with those who have not. The presumption is that cohabiting couples have not yet made a firm and final commitment to be with this partner "till death do us part" or else they would indeed be married. This tentative or partial commitment makes all the difference to their future marriage.

The individuals who live together preceding commitment score more awful after marriage on essentially everything estimated than the people who hold on until marriage or hold on until after engagement. This incorporates:

- Mental hostility

- □Negative collaboration (struggle)
- □Trust in their relationship
- □Conjugal fulfillment
- □Devotion to one another

This risk might be partly explained by the lack of clarity and mutuality of commitment at the time cohabitation begins. The idea of dwelling together assumes the chance of the relationship not working out (and hence the commitment not being extremely durable). In the event that the couple later weds, it tends to be all the more a "sliding into marriage" than a "choosing to wed. As a decision to marry becomes less distinct but more of a gradual slide toward marriage, it blurs the clarity of the commitment.

Despite pay, race, and culture, sliding will be related with more risk than choosing. Deciding will be universally associated with lower risk because of the mutual clarity and resulting follow through. In addition, women are at a greater disadvantage if they move from a cohabiting relationship to marriage. With these couples, husbands have less dedication to their wives than the wives have to their husbands.

2. Keeping the commitment.

"Together forever" can sound so heartfelt - yet it can likewise sound destructive. Whether or not one weds in a common or strict service most couples actually accept that they are are making a permanent commitment. Obviously we as a whole realize that the divorce rate is between 40 -50%, however most couples who wed don't figure it will happen to them. What occurs between the solemn pronouncement of marital promises and the choice to separate? This is certainly not a "one size fits all" circumstance. Certainly some couples made the decision to marry too young, too impetuously, too naively. Others were not mentally mature enough to "spurn all others" or had other person imperfections that were ignored or not apparent during romance. Still others just got exhausted or fed up with attempting to make it work. Still others genuinely worked and did their absolute best to the marriage yet their partner concluded the person in question is wanted out. One can't be married to a missing life partner.

Some spouses must choose the option to leave for their own well being or on the grounds that their life partner won't deal with the marriage. However, r demonstrates the way that numerous relationships could be restored assuming the commitment is solid. Some of the time it is basically the commitment to one another that helps a couple through the harder times, alongside liberal dosages of time, counseling, effort, luck, and faith.

Love is a decision. It reminds couples that however magnificent as the sensation of affection may be, it isn't adequate for a marriage. Sooner or later (really many focuses) a couple need to choose to cherish - in any event, when they don't feel like it. Following up on this choice by doing adoring things for your life partner, talking benevolent and deferentially, and choosing again and again to focus on the relationship makes love rekindle.

Couples who comprehend the quintessence of committing to a long-lasting commitment understand that it's considerably more than simply a choice not to separate. It's a pledge to accomplish the day to day work of keeping the commitment alive. It might mean switching off the TV or going for a daily stroll to pay attention to one another interests. These basic activities, and some more, are the stuff of commitment. They are the activities that keep a marriage dynamic, intriguing, and energizing so compulsions to pursue another decision don't emit.

8. SELFLESSNESS.

Selfishness means to care for only oneself; getting as much as you want but giving little or nothing in return. In short it is all about you.Selfishness is not uncommon because man has a natural tendency to be selfish. In our largely individualistic society, we grow up learning to be selfish, possessive and competitive. Selfishness is a mark of immaturity because it hinders bonding and good fellowship. Selfish people make poor marriage partners and church members because they believe the world revolves around them, and they must have their way all of the time.

We are selfish before marriage.

The truth is, that when you are a solitary unmarried individual you just have one individual to contemplate, yourself. Humans are naturally selfish individuals.

What you need to eat, spots to visit, the music you pay attention to in the vehicle, how to spend your cash, when you did clothing, cleaned your dishes, and so on are everything you in all probability didn't need to consider any other person's perspective or requirements for.

Your needs and wants have come first, and that is a natural response for survival! Who else will take care of these needs for you after you become an independent single adult?

Thinking about your necessities and going to bat for what your ethics are isn't self centered, it makes you what your identity is.

But it all changes after marriage.

The "Single Life" mentality and conduct you had preceding marriage needs to change since you are presently not single. In particular, you are married to the person you want to spend the rest of your life with, your equal partner.

The individual who will plan chicken soup for you when you lay on a wiped out bed (ideally). The individual you will share your most profound delights and distresses with.

After we got married all those “I” statements were changed to “we” or “us“. We had to put each other’s needs above our wants.

We needed to figure out how to think twice about music styles in the vehicle, our food decisions. We needed to settle on the most proficient method to financial plan the cash procured, what we spent it on, the amount to save and so on.

Putting the other individual's necessities before our needs was definitely not a simple interaction, in any case, that is the very thing that we consented to do when we got married.

Considering your accomplice's necessities and wants it critical to blend your lives and think twice about arrangements that work for both of you.

Before marriage, all choices you took were about yourself: what you need; where you went; what you did; what you wore; they generally would in general focus on you. Be that as it may, whenever you're married, the story changes. It is no longer "I" however "We." It is presently not my money yet our money, no longer what I need except for what we want. In marriage, you figure out how to think twice about, marriage changes our discernment and what our qualities ought to be.

The opposite of selfishness is self-denial, humility and generosity.

Although it will never show up on any survey, more marriages are broken up by selfishness than any other reason. Surveys blame it on finances, lack of commitment, infidelity, or incompatibility, but the root cause for most of these reasons is selfishness. A selfish person is committed only to himself or herself, shows little patience, and never learns how to be a successful spouse. Give your hopes, dreams, and life to your partner. And begin to live life together.

This is a simple call to value our marriages, treat them with great care, and invest in them daily. Accomplishing the marriage advice listed above will always require nearly every bit of yourself—but it so worth it if you want to learn how to have a happy marriage.

A successful and healthy marriage is more valuable than most of the temporal things we chase after with our lives. And will always last longer.

Today's world is filled with "me". We tend to see, hear, and look for everything that concerns us. A winning marriage requires selflessness and caring for the other person. When your spouse tells you something, listen. It is that simple.

Turn down your phone, turn off the TV, or stop the car if needed. What is he or she trying to say? Could there be something else? Use your judgment, read between the lines, ask follow-up questions, and write down reminders or notes.

But most importantly, if you are dealing with a difficult situation that involves both of you, turn off your ears about everything related to "you".

Be slow to feel accused or hurt, rather truly try to listen to what your spouse is trying to say.

This can be life-changing for your marriage as well as for your relationships in general.

To be honest, selfishness is human nature. No human could ever claim that they have never behaved selfishly because, at some point in our lives, all of us do.

Now, whether it is in a marriage or any other kind of relationship, selfishness does have a major impact. Particularly in marriage, it can lead to misunderstandings and lack of understanding between the two partners. Wondering how? Let's look at the signs and effects of selfishness, as well as how to get rid of it.

Here are some signs that indicate there is selfishness in marriage.

1. Choices

At the point when an accomplice simply decides and choices that benefit them just, paying little heed to thinking about what it would mean for the other accomplice, then they are envious.

Likewise, it is very self centered of an accomplice in a union with consistently put their longings over the other.

2. Feelings

During slight contentions or a battle, both the accomplices should be circumspect towards one another sentiments. However, it is totally wrong if one partner goes like "Oh, you are hurting my feelings," that is totally selfish of them. What about your partner's feelings? Ask them how they feel about the whole scenario as it is equally important.

3. Career

It is additionally no decent to be lost in your profession while overlooking the time in your marriage. Assuming one accomplice is investing every one of their amounts of energy and time for their vocation, it is to be noticed that they are acting selfishly.

In a marriage, family time ought to be vital, however in the event that one accomplice isn't thinking about it as a significant viewpoint just to make a satisfied future for themselves, then, it is off-base of them.

Here are the consequences of selfishness in marriage-

1. Pushes the partner away

Selfishness leads to distances. At the point when one accomplice is continually demonstrating by their activities that the one in particular that is important to them is their own self, and what they do is in every case right, it makes a confusion in the psyche of the other accomplice.

They believe that their accomplice just needs to stay out of other people's affairs and has no worry for them.

In outrageous cases, most accomplices believe that they hold no worth in their accomplice's life. Subsequently, they begin to become far off and clandestine.

2. Makes the partner feel inferior

Makes the partner feel inferior obviously, when a partner never asks for their spouse's opinions or choices while making a decision, they are bound to feel inferior. It makes them believe that they are not sufficient to have something to do with family matters which is the reason they begin to get peaceful.

3. Disrupts the balance of marriage life

At the point when one is so concerned and consumed in their own self, they neglect to think often about their deep rooted accomplice, their other half. Thinking often about one another need and mind-sets is an essential necessity in marriage. In the event that one can't satisfy that, the marriage will undoubtedly go the incorrect way.

How to overcome selfishness in marriage

So how do you become selfless, instead of selfish in your marriage?

You can accomplish this by preventing that little voice inside from getting you that says:

⇒ But I want my way right now!

⇒ I don't want to wait ….so I will hide it from my spouse.

⇒ I don't want to compromise.

⇒ That's too uncomfortable!

⇒ Their feelings don't make any difference!

Indeed, it sounds extremely youthful when it's worked out so obviously.

Let us clarify, we are not saying your significant other or spouse needs to deny your real necessities. Rather, you ought to both figure out how to place each other's requirements over your needs.
Managing an egotistical life partner can be incredibly troublesome. Yet, have you pondered the times you have been a self centered companion?

Honest conversations and an attitude of responsibility will help you work things out. Regardless of whether you are really at fault for something, don't feel down, irritated, or "the person in question".
Both ought to commit to the responsibility of assuming liability together and consistently support

each other to vanquish any test that might come your direction.

1. Be responsible, and admit that you are selfish.

This is difficult to acknowledge, yet when you know it, conquering selfishness more straightforward. Keep in mind, it's important for what our identity is.

2.Communicate with your life partner about your narrow minded conduct.

Find an equilibrium where you can think twice about alternate on who will pick what.

Express when you feel your companion is being out of line with "I" explanations. "I don't feel appreciated with this choice." OR "I realize you are not doing this to hurt me, however when you X, I feel Y"

This straightforward practice will assist you with building major areas of strength for an and set an extraordinary example for the marriage you both longing.

3. Make decisions together

Settling on a choice ought to continuously include understanding from the two sides. Subsequently, you really want to demonstrate to your mate that their say is similarly pertinent as what you say so nobody feels that they have been forgotten about.

4. Do not make everything about yourself

Do focus on your accomplice. In an argument, inquire as to whether they are alright and in the event that assuming you accidentally put them in an awful mood, apologize before things might deteriorate. Get out of your self-centered bubble and attempt to see things according to your accomplice's perspective.

Assuming you imagine that each wrong thing your accomplice says is pointed towards you, then you are acting selfishly. Continuously becoming guarded and harmed are not the choices. All things being equal, converse with your accomplice about it as nothing works better compared to a useful communication. Significantly impact your mentality. Comprehend that you are presently one. Anything you truly do straightforwardly influence's each other's lives and your marriage. Begin thinking as "WE," not "I.

5. Create a work-life balance

A sound wedded life is only possible when the two accomplices take out time for one another. You ought to have the option to make a cordial and pleasurable second for your accomplice. Additionally, don't just focus in on what you need yet in addition remember their necessities.

These tips ought to have the option to assist you with conquering the evil impacts of selfishness in marriage. Selfishness can make a ton of harm a relationship, you and your accomplice genuinely must recognize and redress the results that selfishness has on your relationship.

6. Eliminate criticism from your relationship

Criticism is a characteristic of toxic relationships. It hurts the connection between the spouses and leads to feelings of inadequacy, low self-esteem, and depression.

The only solution to this is to consciously work on your behavior: how you communicate and act towards your couple when he or she does, thinks, or is something that you disapprove.

We are not saying you should tolerate behaviors like abuse or violence. But in most cases, couples tend to criticize each other for small things, sometimes as stupid as how he brushes his teeth or the type of food she prefers to eat for breakfast.

If something really needs to change in your marriage, you need to talk about it.

If it's not that important just let it go. Your relationship is more important than that.

You don't own your spouse, you are together to enjoy the journey and help each other.

Things will become better when you stop trying to change or improve your spouse's tiny details.

The truth is that couples that practice self-improvement and work with couple goals will eventually solve any small (or big) details about themselves and their marriage because their mind is always set to become the best version of themselves.

Stop being competitive with each other. You are a team. So work on how you can bring out the best in each other.

7. Eliminate bracing for the victim position when arguments come up.

This one is extremely clear, yet not exceptionally practiced in many relationships.

It comes to what we recently referenced about focusing in on "me" as it were.

At the point when argument comes up, or even a discussion about progress, don't feel accused.

What's more, assuming that you were accused, don't strike back!

8.Remember you can't transform anybody yet yourself

Remember you can’t change anyone but yourself

So work on you and keep the communication channel open with your spouse about what you're learning.

Improve yourself, and if you are in a happy and healthy relationship your spouse will follow suit. Thinking of your needs and standing up for what your morals are is not selfish, it's what makes you who you are.

You also have to stand up for your actual needs like time alone. Otherwise, you are creating a very unhealthy relationship where you deny yourself completely and will lose yourself.

9. Serve your spouse.

How can you help your spouse today? What service can you do to make your spouse's life easier today?

Maybe it's washing the dishes, folding the laundry, or taking the garbage even though it's not your turn to do it.

More importantly, make a difference in their life today!

As you already know, money plays a huge role in our lives and can be the reason why you have selfish behaviors. So spend some time to review the root cause of all your money problems this week, if not today.

For instance:

Would you like to spend more cash on your needs rather than the necessities of your home?

Do you believe you merit more "spending dollars" or have a "greater say" on how cash is spent in light of the fact that you are the sole/higher worker in your marriage?

Might it be said that you are concealing the legacy, the additional reward you got working, or the additional spending Simply answering the questions above is a great way to start working on overcoming selfishness in your marriage and opening up communication. Because your answers will tell you whether you are being selfish or not. Is it all about you?

Next, share your answers and thoughts about the questions with your spouse. Have a conversation, and create an action plan to ensure your selfish behavior with money or whatever topic can stop.

If necessary, make a month to month financial plan to follow your pay and costs together, regardless of whether you have joint ledgers.

By successfully practicing how to not be selfish with money, you will be able to start changing your selfish behaviors. Your mindset will change from always thinking about “Me” to “Us”.

Taking care of oneself is not selfish.

To become magnanimous and not selfish in your marriage, begin by rejecting that little voice inside you that says, "I ought to have all that I need, when I need it, and how I need it."

CONCLUSION

We consider love an inclination, yet we don't necessarily comprehend that showing that feeling is so important. "As a relationship goes on, it requires to a greater degree a cognizant work to ask yourself, How could I show my accomplice my adoration today?" That could mean composing your better half an affection note, giving him a foot rub following an extreme day, getting his hand during a walk, or getting his number one frozen yogurt returning. "It's simply simple, easily overlooked details that say, 'Hello, I'm considering you and your joy. After some time, those things amount to convey, 'I love you, I care about you, and I'm glad that we're together.

Try not to hold on until you get into a monstrous battle to air every one of your complaints, so, all in all things will generally get dramatically overemphasized or disregarded in the aftermath. One time per week or somewhere in the vicinity, ask your accomplice, 'Is there anything I've done recently that is caused distance between us? We need to realize that our accomplice is keen on our sentiments — even hurt or upset ones. In any case, your significant other may not be accustomed to broadcasting his feelings in quiet discussion, so permit him an opportunity to think before you leave and continue on with your day. You're allowing your significant other to empty his kept sentiments in a decent, protected, delicate way, which he could not usually have the valuable chance to do

Regardless of whether you're mindful of it, long periods of attempting to keep a reasonable marriage can prompt a sort of rivalry between accomplices. "That quiet score-keeping of who works more, who's more drained, who does more tasks, who will spend time with companions more, who spends more cash, who has all the more available energy, and so forth. Regardless of whether you're not grumbling without holding back, developed disdain will influence each part of your coexistence. "Marriage is a group sport."If somebody's triumphant, you're not kidding." Pursue a day to day choice to destroy that score sheet — and keep intellectually destroying it consistently until it becomes propensity.

The main words harder to say than "I love you" may very well be "Please accept my apologies." Nobody likes to concede they were off-base, and once in a while a statement of regret can want to surrender shortcoming or rout. Be that as it may, several gets into it incidentally, and can we just be real — nobody individual can be correct constantly.

Recollecting that your relationship is a higher priority than being correct, this is urgent to keeping a decent marriage. Every so often, on the off chance that it's a dumb battle or it doesn't mean much to the master plan, be the one to say, 'Hello, Please accept my apologies as far as it matters for me in this conflict. Our marriage implies more to me than winning this contention.'"

You know when you request that your better half follow through with something, he doesn't, then, at that point, months go by and the hatred just endlessly constructs? That is unpleasant for both of you. Request what you need when your accomplice could really do it for you. While you bring something up at a second when it could never get achieved. Then you quit asking, begin pushing your need away from view, and it turns into a thing. "Asking at the perfect time makes you a more effective couple by showing your life partner that you regard his time and are focusing on her needs and needs, as well.

In our occupied, surged world, closeness can at times go by the wayside. A great deal of that obligation falls on spouses, from whom we frequently anticipate heartfelt shocks or terrific motions. In any case, don't hang tight for him to take action. Fire things up with an unconstrained, energetic kiss or bring back pastry and blossoms. Your significant other needs to realize you're keen on him truly; that is similarly as large a thing for men for all intents and purposes for ladies." And both of you will receive the benefits.

At long last, there are numerous relationships in a marriage. This is on the grounds that a marriage is comprised of numerous mistake, trailed by numerous important times of development and mending - and most pardoning - followed again by unavoidable new frustrations.

Quite possibly of the main thing you can do to further develop your marriage is to comprehend what love and marriage truly is - a battle for two questionable and frequently desolate individuals not to relinquish the other's hand as they clear their path through the whole excursion that life has set before them.

I wish you all the best as you and your partner make your own journey!

www.ingramcontent.com/pod-product-compliance
Lightning Source LLC
LaVergne TN
LVHW010550160826
845677LV00013B/3076